Bridging the Gap

12 Ways to Connect With Your Child

SINDY AUGUSTIN

Published by:
Sindy Augustin
Fort-Lauderdale, Florida

Bridging the Gap: 12 Ways to Connect With Your Child

Copyright ©2021 Sindy Augustin
ISBN- 978-1-7364364-0-0

Unless noted otherwise, Scripture quotations are from The Holy Bible, King James Version(KJV, New King James Version (NKJV), Message Version (MSGV), and English Standard Version(ESV).
© 1994 by Thomas Nelson, Inc.

ALL RIGHTS RESERVED

No part of this book may be reproduced in any form or by any electronic or mechanical means, including information storage and retrieval systems, without permission in writing from the publisher, except by reviewers, who may quote brief passages in a review.

FOR INFORMATION:
WWW.SINDYSPEAKS.COM

Printed in the United States of America

Dedication

Bridging the Gap:12 Ways to Connect With Your Child is dedicated to God first and foremost. He has given me the inspiration and determination to encourage parents and their children not to lose hope in a season where there is so much uncertainty. Despite it all, there is hope in staying connected with your child on this journey called life.

To my loving sons Daron A. Eugene, for making sure that you always do your best to understand the "why's" of being a child in its totality. To Donovan E. Eugene, my youngest, thank you for creating ways the family can unite by never letting any one of us lose focus on what's important to usall.

And to my readers, thank you in advance. Thank you for the outpouring of testimonials and support, which will contribute to this book's success.

Table of Contents

Foreword 7

Introduction 9

Step 1 11
   Take Time to Communicate

Step 2 29
   Take Time to Actively Listen

Step 3 47
   Take Time to Learn

Step 4 65
   Take Time to Understand

Step 5 83
   Take the Time to Model

Step 6 101
   Take the Time to Teach

Step 7 119
   Take the Time to Support

Step 8 137
   Take the Time to Validate

Step 9   **155**
    Take the Time to Invest

Step 10   **173**
    Take the Time to Inspire

Step 11   **191**
    Take the time to Balance

Step 12   **209**
    Take the Time to Unite

Conclusion   **227**

About The Author   **231**

Other Titles By Author   **233**

Foreword

Despite popular belief, good parenting doesn't always come naturally. You may have a desire to do better than your parents did, and the idea of that is commendable. However, what I know as a Clinician is that if you don't learn new ways of completing a task, you will resort to what you know. This book is outlined for easy reading and reference. It gives you simple tools that you can begin implementing immediately and efficiently. This book provides you with a canvas, brush, and paint to create what you would have desired your family to become. I guarantee you will see a difference in how you and your children relate. How am I so sure? It worked for me.

— MAGDA DEMERITT, MSW, LCSW

In times of distress, some people take the position of Protestor; noting all things out of order in a system, but offering no solution. Others like Dr. Sindy become Activists, not just recognizing the issues but creating a plan to deal with them. Her passion for seeing the next generation excel by bridging the communicative and educational gaps between parents and children is unmatched. It's been a pleasure seeing this project come to fruition.

— SHAUN TOMBLIN, BRAND STRATEGIST, AND MENTOR

Dr. Sindy has a voice that matters and is one who God has called to be to be the voice of many, especially the youth of the world. In this book of wisdom, her voice echoes the longing of a need for parents to effectively communicate with their child(ren) for the overall key development and instructional life training of a child. She does not just identify the problems of ineffective parent-child relationship, but she provides a solution, which she has developed through her varied experiences as a mother, teacher, counselor and church youth leader."

— NEKISHIA LESTER, ESQ.

Introduction

Hello, this is Dr. Sindy. Through my journey of being a parent and a child to my parents, I realized that the art of parenting is truly a lifetime commitment and process. We have often observed, believed, and applied a myriad of parenting strategies that may or may not work simply because everyone's situation is different.

I was born in the "70s in Miami, Florida. Although I was born in the United States of America, my upbringing was deeply rooted in the Haitian culture. More specifically, we are a people that believe children are seen and not heard. We believe that if you had a girl child, she had to learn how to cook as early as 6 years old or even younger. If you had a male child, he had to learn how to use his hands in the land or do whatever they considered manly. So, learning how to cook, clean, and care for others was engraved in my mind at a very early age.

Now, one would think that was a huge responsibility for a child who has not even fully developed, right? I agree with you one hundred percent. However, it does not change the reality that these cultural systems of raising children are a part of how we, ourselves, parent our own children. Unless we take a moment and evaluate the parenting values and systems that we were exposed to growing up, we will not recognize the patterns that do not align with our own definition of parenting now that we have children of our own. Over the years, I had to challenge my parenting style to ensure I was not repeating the cycle of dysfunction or the behaviors that I do not believe align with the values I have grown to cherish now that I am a parent.

Over the years of parenting, I realize there are twelve areas of parenting that are critical in every stage of a child's life. This book looks at those areas that are often the most challenging during one of the many developmental stages of any child. The art of parenting requires establishing healthy relationships between parent and child through practical strategies when they are in elementary school. With every challenge parent's face, there is a problem, a solution, and the reality of that situation. Knowing the problem is half the battle. Having a solution and gaining a reality check helps put things into perspective is excellent as well. However, reading a real-life story on putting all three together is the icing on the cake.

I pray that reading Bridging the Gap: 12 Ways to Connect With Your Child unlocks your mind and heart. When this happens ,you will gain the determination needed to put in everything you have learned into working in partnership with your child on this journey called life.

Step 1

Take Time to Communicate

"Do as I say, not as I do."

My Story: While driving home with my boys one afternoon, I was exhausted from a long day of work. They were busy in the back being children—laughing, joking around and just being noisy in the car. While on the phone, the boys decided that horse playing in the car's back seat was a great idea. In my mind, I could not understand why this was happening, mostly when they knew making noise while I'm on the phone was a big NO-NO! As a result of my fatigue, disbelief, and inability to hear the person on the phone, I snapped at and chastised them.

The chastisement would not have been a problem if the tone of my voice had been different. Once done, I continued talking as though nothing ever happened. At some point, as I continued the conversation, I realized that I was out of order. So I asked the caller to hold on while apologizing to them for yelling like a madwoman. I did not want them to misinterpret my frustration with their behavior to them as an individual.

I took the time to explain to them that what they did was disrespectful for many reasons. The first was because I was on the phone. The second was because they knew the rules when they see an adult on the phone. Finally, it was because they chose to ignore my signals requesting them to stop the horse playing in the back. Once I finished explaining to them how they were disrespectful, I also acknowledged that I was rude. Although I was annoyed and disappointed in their actions, how I corrected their behavior was discourteous. As a result, I asked for their forgiveness, and they did the same for me.

Problem: Frequently, as parents, we tend to believe that our children do not understand us. The challenge is when we spend much time convincing them to do as we say while forgetting, they observe what we are doing instead. When this happens, our children tune us out or become unresponsive, which makes the situation worse. As a result, the words we use push them away instead of pulling them closer to us. Expecting them to stay tuned in when we are not communicating with them in a manner that teaches them how to respond to us appropriately is ineffective. There are two types of communication. The first one is verbal, which is communication expressed through words. The second one is nonverbal communication, told through body language, gestures, or facial expressions.

Solution: Take the time necessary to get to know which communication style works best for your child. Identifying what you have observed as their preferred style of communication will help you connect with them where they are instead of where you expect them to be. Just because they are younger than we are and are dependent upon us does not mean that it is okay to disrespect them. Depending on the culture, this can have a lasting adverse effect on children during their elementary years. Speaking to a child that promotes respect, understanding, and intentional listening will give you the far better results you expect to see over time. Though it is a process that requires intentionality and consistency, it is worth the investment.

Reality: It is necessary for us as parents to invest the time required to teach our children appropriate ways to express themselves. To achieve this, it is essential to teach and model effective communication techniques both inside and outside the home. Remember that their character and behavior will ALWAYS resemble their training or not receiving at home. If we teach our children that yelling, cursing, or shutting down is the best method of communicating, this is what they are going to give us. However, if we teach them and practice with them how to effectively communicate regardless of the situation, conversation, or atmosphere, we can expect better results.

Sometimes that may require that you, as the parent, apologize, change your tone, or even humble yourself around your child when you speak. Do understand; this does not minimize your authority as a parent. Instead, it shows your child that you are mature enough to accept your mistakes and can assume full responsibility for them as well. Are your actions as a parent communicating love, joy, peace, long suffering, gentleness, goodness, faith, meekness, and temperance (see Galatians 5:22-23)? Are your actions communicating and provoking your children to anger (see Ephesians 6:4)? What are you going to do to change it and how?

What's Your Story?

Journal
from your heart

"Speaking to a child in a manner that promotes respect, understanding, and intentional listening will give you far better results."

— **Dr. Sindy**

Step 1

Take Time to Communicate

"CAN YOU HEAR ME NOW?"

Week 1

Think About This

Are your actions as a parent promoting that relationship you believe to be healthy according to your own values? Are your actions communicating and provoking your children to respond in a manner that is not in alignment with your core values or belief systems? If not, what are you going to do to change it? How are you going to change it? After reflecting on the questions above which deals with taking time to communicate, today, sit down in a quiet place and write the top two problems you are facing as it relates to you in this area. Jot down two solutions you are willing to apply immediately to get the results you desire. Then write down what might get in your way from realistically applying the standards you already set in place.

Problem

1. _____
   _____
   _____
   _____

2. _____
   _____
   _____
   _____

Solution

1. _____
   _____
   _____
   _____

2. _____
   _____
   _____
   _____

Reality

_____
_____
_____
_____
_____
_____

Your Declaration

Today, I declare
that I no longer have
communication
problems with my child(ren).
As a parent,
I will commit to communicating with
my child(ren) in a manner
that promotes,
love, understanding and respect.
As a result,
the manner in which we communicate with one another
is alignment with our family values.

Day 1

> "When we change the way we communicate, we change society"
> ~ **Clay Shirky**

Tonight as I sit down and reflect on how I communicated with my child(ren), I can honestly say that I

___

> **Proverbs 15:2** ~ The tongue of the wise uses knowledge aright: but the mouth of fools pours out foolishness. **(NKJV)**

Tonight as I sit down and reflect on how I communicated with my child(ren), I can honestly say that I

___
___
___
___
___
___
___
___
___
___
___
___
___
___
___
___
___

> "The most important thing in communication is hearing what isn't said."
> ~ **Peter Drucker**

Tonight as I sit down and reflect on how I communicated with my child(ren), I can honestly say that I

Ephesians 4:29 – Let no corrupt word proceed out of your mouth, but what is good for necessary edification that it may impart grace to the hearers. **(NKJV)**

Tonight as I sit down and reflect on how I communicated with my child(ren), I can honestly say that I

> "Nothing lowers the level of conversation more than raising the voice."
> ~ **Stanley Horowitz**

Tonight as I sit down and reflect on how I communicated with my child(ren), I can honestly say that I

_____
_____
_____
_____
_____
_____
_____
_____
_____
_____
_____
_____
_____
_____
_____
_____
_____
_____

> **Psalm 141:3** - Set a guard, O Lord, over my mouth; keep watch over the door of my lips! **(NIV)**

Tonight as I sit down and reflect on how I communicated with my child(ren), I can honestly say that I

Day 7

> "Constantly talking isn't necessarily communicating."
> ~ **Charlie Kaufman**

Tonight as I sit down and reflect on how I communicated with my child(ren), I can honestly say that I

Step 2

Take Time to Actively Listen

"Hearing + Connecting = Success?"

My Story: Given the various functions of my life, I can honestly say, at times, active and intentional listening can be a challenge. There are times when I am so exhausted from the demands of my life outside of the home that I have no energy mentally or physically to even engage in conversation with my children. It wasn't until my boys told me how much they missed connecting with me as their mother that I realized a shift needed to occur. They said, "mom, you are now always so busy; we never have time to talk anymore." Imagine your elementary age son or daughter communicating their truth to you in this manner, and you miss it. That reality of not being heard or having their feelings validated could push them in the wrong direction.

You see, they'd see me on conference calls, personal and or business calls often. Not having access to connecting led them to believe that these calls or conversations were more important to me compared to listening to them. Regardless of how busy my day is, I now make sure the first thing I do when I get home is to listen to my children's stories of their days. If I know I will arrive home when they are sleeping, I ensure I make time out to call them and talk. Scheduling family time for us to go out and connect was necessary as well. If we (as parents) do not make connecting with our children a priority to us, trust and believe that someone else whom we do not approve of will.

Problem: Many parents do not believe children should have a voice or a right to speak and express themselves; they believe children should be seen and not heard. Depending on when and where you were born, you may or may not subscribe to this philosophy. In some cases, I believe this is true; however, not all the time. When a child is repeatedly ignored or disengaged with their parents, that child may result in searching for someone or something to hear them out. Furthermore, this same child may turn to the streets, their friends, television, or the many social media platforms out there in hopes of being heard or engaged. Listening to your child(ren) as a parent needs to be a priority regardless of how busy life demands become.

Solution: Regardless of how busy we are as parents remaining uninterested in listening or engaging with our child(ren) will result in unnecessary arguments, battles, or frustrations. Take the time needed to listen to what your child is saying or not saying around you. Pay attention to their discussions with their friends, siblings, or even when they talk to you. Ask questions and prepare yourself for the answers they may give. Make it you business to get them to describe their day at school, on the bus, at lunch, or whatever extracurricular activity they participate in.

As you begin connecting with their day through active listening, you will identify their thought process. It also allows you to catch alarming information that they may not have intended to share with you for one reason or another. The more you pay attention to what your child is saying, the better you will become at helping him or her through challenging situations. Another great tip is scheduling bonding time outside of the everyday routine. This bonding time involves getting dressed, going out, or simply engaging in activities you both enjoy. This bonding moment should include you and your child. If you have more than one child, the process is the same. You will create experiences and memories of the two of you enjoying one another's company.

Reality: In today's society, it is tough being a child. The struggles our children are facing today is nothing like what we dealt with growing up. For one thing, the school system is a lot harder and more challenging. The restrictions of not being able to socialize in a more suitable way to their personality are even more challenging. Although there are more advantages and resources available to them to stay connected remotely, their demands are outrageous. There were days my boys would bring very confusing homework home. I felt defeated because I could not even assist with providing clarification to increase understanding. Not because I was incompetent, but because of other factors. They could not bring their book home, or the book did not have real examples to go by, and soon.

The challenges we face daily can and will drain us that we do not have the time or energy to listen attentively or engage in conversation with our children. When was the last time you sat down and had a heart-to-heart conversation that your child? Does your child feel like he or she can talk to you about anything without being judged? If you do not know, what are you going to do to change that? There is much value to gain when you take the time to listen to your child(ren).

What's Your Story?

Journal
from your heart

"The more you pay attention to what your child is saying, the better you will become at helping him or her through challenging situations."

~ **Dr. Sindy**

Step 2

Take Time to Listen

"HEARING + CONNECTING = SUCCESS"

Week 2

Think About This

When was the last time you sat down and had a heart- to-heart conversation with your child? Does your child feel like he or she can talk to you about anything without being judged? If you do not know, what are you going to do to change that? There is much value when you (the parent) take time to listen to them (your child). After reflecting on the questions above which deals with taking time to listen, today, sit down in a quiet place and write the top two problems you are facing as it relates to you in this area. Jot down two solutions you are willing to apply immediately to get the results you desire. Then write down what might get in your way from realistically applying the standards you already set in place.

Problem

1. _____
   _____
   _____
   _____
   _____

2. _____
   _____
   _____
   _____
   _____

Solution

1. _____
   _____
   _____
   _____
   _____

2. _____
   _____
   _____
   _____
   _____

Reality

_____
_____
_____
_____
_____
_____

Your Declaration

Today, I declare
that I will no longer
divide my attention
when my child(ren) is/are trying
to have a conversation with me.
I will give them
my undivided attention when
they are speaking to me
because what they have to say
is important and
their thoughts and feelings
matter to me.

> "An open ear is the only believable sign of an open heart."
> ~ **David Augsburger**

Tonight as I sit down and reflect on how I listened to my child(ren), I can honestly say that today I

Proverbs 18:13 ~ He who answers a matter before he hears it, it is folly and shame to him. **(NKJV)**

Tonight as I sit down and reflect on how I listened to my child(ren), I can honestly say that today I

Day 3

> "In the practice of our days, to listen is to lean in, softly, with a willingness to be changed by what we hear." ~ **Mark Nepo**

Tonight as I sit down and reflect on how I listened to my child(ren), I can honestly say that today I

_____
_____
_____
_____
_____
_____
_____
_____
_____
_____
_____
_____
_____
_____
_____
_____
_____
_____

John 10:27 ~ My sheep listen to my voice; I know them, and they follow me. **(NIV)**

Tonight as I sit down and reflect on how I listened to my child(ren), I can honestly say that today I

Day 5

> "Courage is what it takes to stand up and speak; courage is also what it takes to sit down and listen."
> ~ **Winston Churchill**

Tonight as I sit down and reflect on how I listened to my child(ren), I can honestly say that today I

_____
_____
_____
_____
_____
_____
_____
_____
_____
_____
_____
_____
_____
_____
_____
_____
_____
_____
_____
_____

Proverbs 1:33 ~ But whoever listens to me will live in safety and be at ease, without fear of harm. **(NIV)**

Tonight as I sit down and reflect on how I listened to my child(ren), I can honestly say that today I

> "Before I can tell my life what I want to do with it, I must listen to my life telling me who I am."
> ~ **Parker J. Palmer**

Tonight as I sit down and reflect on how I listened to my child(ren), I can honestly say that today I

___
___
___
___
___
___
___
___
___
___
___
___
___
___
___
___
___

Step 3
Take Time to Learn

"NEVER JUDGE A BOOK BY ITS COVER."

My Story: One day, while grocery shopping, the boys saw a former classmate from a program that they participated in over the summer. They were so excited and proceeded to greet the young man in a way that I did not expose them to. I was shocked, not because they greeted their friend inappropriately, rather because I've never seen that side of them before. When they saw me, they quickly conformed to what they believed was congruent to my family values.

I took this experience and turned it into a teachable moment for us all. I explained to my sons how I valued their individuality and collectively as children. I also expressed how I wanted to see them for who they were at all times, regardless of where they were. I further said how this allowed me to teach and guide them through those difficult times I knew they would face one day as young men. I encouraged them to live authentically at all times, both inside and outside the home.

Problem: As a parent, take time to learn and get acquainted with your child's spirit and behavior. As an educator, I realize the tendency to train children to behave a certain acceptable way, without realizing when they are not in our presence that their behavior is entirely the opposite, at times. Not allowing children the space to discover their true authentic selves will lead them down a path of confusion. The result of this confusion will produce a conflict in their emotions and belief that their true self is not worthy of being displayed around their parents. They are left to believe that they must conform to a perfect child's standards to be accepted by their parents and others.

Solution: Create an atmosphere that will allow your children to be themselves. If their behaviors, actions, or conversations are out of line with your beliefs, values, or morals as parents, take the time out to get to their core issues. In every behavior, action, or reaction, a seed planted sprouted a root to it all. So you must take the time out to do your research and investigate when, where, how, and possibly what triggered that particular behavior. Also, take the time to learn what makes your child happy, sad, upset, irritated, uncomfortable, threatened, etc. You can achieve this through role-play or during heart-to-heart conversations.

Reality: If we as parents do not take the time to get to know our children, we will lose out on so many opportunities to help, defend, support, understand, or even enjoy who they are as individuals. Think of a doctor who just met a new patient. In the beginning, all they know is what the patient tells them via the "New Patient Questionnaire." Keep in mind; the patient is the one in control of giving the doctor what he/she needs to formulate an understanding of who that patient is. However, it is not until the doctor takes the time to speak with the patient over time will he/she get a better understanding of the patient's needs. The patient has to make it their business to get to know the doctor as well.

As parents, we must take the same proactive approach in learning our children from the inside to the outside. Do you know what your child likes? Do you know their favorite color, dinner, animal, sport, snack, dessert, subject in school, or favorite music type? If not, how are you going to change that? When you (the parent) take the time to learn more about them (your child), your love for each other will strengthen as a result.

What's Your Story?

Journal
from your heart

"When you (the parent) take the time to learn more about them (your child) your love for each other will strengthen as a result."

~ Dr. Sindy

Step 3

Take Time to Learn

"NEVER JUDGE A BOOK BY ITS COVER"

Week 3

Think About This

Do you know what your child really likes? Do you know what is his/her favorite color, dinner, animal, sport, snack, desert, school subject or favorite music? If not, how are you going to change that? When you (the parent) take the time to learn more about them (your child) your love for each other will strengthen as a result. After reflecting on the questions above which deals with taking time to learn, today, sit down in a quiet place and write the top two problems you are facing as it relates to you in this area. Jot down two solutions you are willing to apply immediately to get the results you desire. Then write down what might get in your way from realistically applying the standards you already set in place.

Problem

1. _____

2. _____

Solution

1. _____

2. _____

Reality

_____
_____
_____
_____
_____
_____

Your Declaration

Today, I declare
that I will take the time
to learn more about my child(ren).
As a parent,
I will commit to really discovering
what my child(ren) favorite show(s),
movies, food, games, sports, music,
desert, colors, style, and more with
patience, love and understanding.
As a result,
our relationship will strengthen.

> "In learning you will teach, and in teaching you will learn."
> ~ **Phil Collins**

Tonight as I sit down and reflect on one thing I learned about my child(ren), I can honestly say that I

Proverbs 1:5 ~ A wise man will hear and increase learning, and a man of understanding will attain wise counsel, **(NKJV)**

Tonight as I sit down and reflect on one thing I learned about my child(ren), I can honestly say that I

Day 3

> We learn from failure, not from success.
> ~ **Bram Stoker**

Tonight as I sit down and reflect on one thing I learned about my child(ren), I can honestly say that I

_____

_____

_____

_____

_____

_____

_____

_____

_____

_____

_____

_____

_____

_____

_____

_____

_____

_____

_____

Proverbs 18:15 ~ Wise men and women are always learning, always listening for fresh insight. **(MSG)**

Tonight as I sit down and reflect on one thing I learned about my child(ren), I can honestly say that I

> "Live as if you were to die tomorrow. Learn as if you were to live forever."
> ~ **Mahatma Gandhi**

Tonight as I sit down and reflect on one thing I learned about my child(ren), I can honestly say that I

___

Proverbs 1:7 ~ The fear of the Lord is the beginning of knowledge; fools despise wisdom and instruction. **(NKJV)**

Tonight as I sit down and reflect on one thing I learned about my child(ren), I can honestly say that I

> "Educating the mind without educating the heart is no education at all."
> ~ **Aristotle**

Tonight as I sit down and reflect on one thing I learned about my child(ren), I can honestly say that I

Step 4

Take Time to Understand

"Parents just don't understand."

My Story: I remember when I made the tough decision to remove my sons from the public school system here in South Florida. They were enrolled in the private school system to shield them from the daily challenges children tend to deal with in public school. The process of searching for the school that would be the best fit was long and challenging. Though the private school system provided many excellent opportunities the public school did not offer; my eldest son still dealt with some of the same challenges I was desperately trying to protect him from. I failed to realize that regardless of what school the children attended, challenges would be there. Challenges such as bullying, cursing, and other behaviors that he knew were inappropriate.

It may not have been at the same magnitude as those found at the public school, but the challenges were still there. My oldest son would now come home from school upset or behaving, unlike his usual self. Because this is not his normal behavior, I instantly knew something was wrong. Instead of yelling at him because he was being rude or yelling at his brother, I pulled him aside and talked with him. Why? Because I saw past the outward behavior and dealt with the root of his actions when the challenges surfaced immediately, the outcome was far more positive and promising. There is no way I could have supported or assisted him through this process. My communication lines with my sons did not exist.

Problem: Children often believe that no one sincerely cares about or understands the challenges they deal with every moment of the day. Social media continuously attack their minds, eyes, and ears, making it exceptionally difficult for them to focus in school, on homework, or during their exams. These distractions and challenges frequently hinder their decisions to do what they know to be right. Fear also saturates the streets we live in more than ever before. Fear of the unknown, death, bullying, exams, rejection, and more can be challenging to deal with when a child believes no one understands them.

Solution: Sit back and consider all the factors that can hinder your child's success daily. Look at the environment they are in from when they leave their homes safely and consider ALL those factors. Ride the bus with them if possible. Walk the hallways with them if possible. Look at the bathrooms they are using daily or the cafeteria they are eating in. Look at the playgrounds they are playing on or the field they have physical education on. Look at the route(s) they take when walking to and from school. Better yet, look at the other people who are on that same route. Doing this will give you a better understanding of what your child encounters daily.

Reality: Take time to get to know your children. Please take off the parental lens and see your child for who they are and not whom they are forcing themselves to be around you. Try putting yourself in their shoes and walk a day in their life. It was not until we consciously decided to look at what our children were dealing with daily that we understood why their behaviors and actions fluctuated at times. Ask them whole-heartedly and sincerely why they decided to do what they did, considering the other favorable options available to them.

This step is critical to breaking the barriers between you (the parent) and them (your children). This step helps you to understand their thought process as well. Have you taken the shades off your eyes to see your child for who he/she is and not as whom you want to see? Does your child ever express the joy he/she feels because he/she knows you understand him/her? If not, what are you going to do about it? It will be advantageous for you to understand your child to bridge the connecting gap present in the relationship between both of you.

What's Your Story?

Journal

from your heart

"Your pride can be the number barrier to understanding the flaws in your relationship with your child."

~ **Dr. Sindy**

Step 4

Take Time to Understand

"PARENTS JUST DON'T UNDERSTAND"

Week 4

Think About This

Have you taken the shades off your eyes to see your child for who he/she really is and not as whom you want to see as? Does your child ever express the joy he/she feels because he/she knows you understand him/her? If not, what are you going to do about it? It is truly important for you (the parent) to take the time to understand your child if you wish to better the relationship between the both of you. After reflecting on the questions above which deals with taking time to understand, today, sit down in a quiet place and write the top two problems you are facing as it relates to you in this area. Jot down two solutions you are willing to apply immediately to get the results you desire. Then write down what might get in your way from realistically applying the standards you already set in place.

Problem

1. _____
   _____
   _____
   _____

2. _____
   _____
   _____
   _____

Solution

1. _____
   _____
   _____
   _____

2. _____
   _____
   _____
   _____

Reality

_____
_____
_____
_____
_____
_____
_____

Your Declaration

Today, I declare that
I no longer have
a challenge understanding my child(ren).
As a parent,
my child(ren) needs to trust
me first and that is important to me.
As a result,
my behavior, attitude and response
when challenges, struggles or trials come,
will always promote understanding, trust and love.

> **Proverbs 18:2** ~ A fool takes no pleasure in understanding, but only in expressing his opinion. **(NIV)**

Tonight as I sit down and reflect on my responses or reactions to my child(ren)s' behavior, I can honestly say

> "Everything that irritates us about others can lead us to an understanding of ourselves."
> ~ **Carl Jung**

Tonight as I sit down and reflect on my responses or reactions to my child(ren)s' behavior, I can honestly say

___

Proverbs 15:14 ~ The heart of him who has understanding seeks knowledge, but the mouth of fools feeds on foolishness. **(NKJV)**

Tonight as I sit down and reflect on my responses or reactions to my child(ren)s' behavior, I can honestly say

___

> "Understanding is the first step to acceptance, and only with acceptance can there be recovery."
> ~ **J.K. Rowling**

Tonight as I sit down and reflect on my responses or reactions to my child(ren)s' behavior, I can honestly say

___
___
___
___
___
___
___
___
___
___
___
___
___
___
___
___
___
___
___

> **Proverbs 14:29** ~ Slowness to anger makes for deep understanding; a quick-tempered person stockpiles stupidity. **(MSG)**

Tonight as I sit down and reflect on my responses or reactions to my child(ren)s' behavior, I can honestly say

> "Nothing in life is to be feared. It is only to be understood."
> ~ **Marie Curie**

Tonight as I sit down and reflect on my responses or reactions to my child(ren)s' behavior, I can honestly say

Proverbs 3:13 ~ Happy is the man who finds wisdom, and the man go gains understanding. **(NKJV)**

Tonight as I sit down and reflect on my responses or reactions to my child(ren)s' behavior, I can honestly say

___
___
___
___
___
___
___
___
___
___
___
___
___
___
___
___
___
___

Step 5

Take the Time to Model

"Do as I say, not as I do!"

My Story: It was a daily hassle to get my oldest son to put his seatbelt on in the car. I would demand, yell, and even chastise him for not being obedient to the directions given to him, until one day when he spoke up. He said, "Mom, you always say for us to put our seat belts on, but you and dad don't always put your seat belts on." It was not until that moment that I realized he was not listening to what I was saying but watching what I was displaying. Immediately I knew I was in error and had to reevaluate my process. I began ensuring what I said matched my behavior ALWAYS. When it did not, I made the necessary changes immediately because of their perception of me as their mom, a person, and their mentor mattered more than my pride. Furthermore, I did not want my actions to continue confusing them as it did in the past.

Problem: It is not very clear for a child to behave or respond in a certain way when their parent speaks and acts oppositely. We tell them to listen when speaking, but they do not receive the same courtesy in return. We tell them that certain behaviors are wrong such as gossiping, lying, procrastination, cursing, or rude behaviors, to name a few. However, we turn around and do the same things our selves.

Solution: Take the time to show or model the behaviors that consistently align with what you hold to be true. Sit down with your children and talk about your relationship with them as a parent. Ask them what things they like and dislike about the family relationship. Understand that children pay close attention to all of the signs we and the world are sending their way. Be ready to hear the brutal truth that needs to be said.

Because you want the truth, this would not be the time to argue, fuss, or take things personally. Instead, this is the time to model problem-solving skills, the right way to communicate, and other vital developmental strategies that they need to learn from you as a parent. Regardless of your faith or belief, this can be incorporated into your home. There are countless resources online and books you can pick up at the local library in your area to help you with challenges in this area. There are YouTube channels, podcasts, or even online groups you can follow to connect with a community of parents like yourself. I highly recommend reading *Parenting Beyond Your Capacity: Connect Your Family to a Wider Community* by Reggie Joyner and *Parenting by the Book: Biblical Wisdom to Raising Your Child* by John Rosemond. Both books provide you with biblical and practical approaches to solving challenges experienced through parenting.

Reality: Our children learn the right or wrong things from us. We are in a century where children want and need to see it before they can even attempt to believe it. They are watching with a naked eye to everything thrown their way, whether verbal, physical, or non- verbal. As parents, if we don't modify such behaviors as we acknowledge our wrongs and asking for forgiveness, we will miss out on many opportunities to teach valuable lessons.

Choose to take those negative responses or behaviors and turn them into teachable moments. Identify the problem and model the right way of handling those communication challenges. This will show them that you acknowledge that you are not perfect and you make mistakes too. When was the last time you apologized to your child for offending them or reacting inappropriately? When was the last time you took the time to explain your child's decision to provide him/her with a better understanding of your actions? If you have not done this, how are you going to start? Chose to show them that your love for them is more profound than the situation or challenge at hand.

What's Your Story?

Journal

from the heart

"Take the time to show or model the behaviors that consistently align with what you hold to be true."

~ Dr. Sindy

Step 5

Take Time to Model

"Do as I say, not as I do!"

Week 5

Think About This

When was the last time you apologized to your child for offending them or reacting inappropriately? When was the last time you took the time to explain your decision to your child in order to provide him/her with a better understanding of your actions? If you have not done this, how are you going to start? After reflecting on the questions above which deals with taking time to model, today, sit down in a quiet place and write the top two problems you are facing as it relates to you in this area. Jot down two solutions you are willing to apply immediately to get the results you desire. Then write down what might get in your way from realistically applying the standards you already set in place.

Problem

1. _____
   _____
   _____
   _____
   _____

2. _____
   _____
   _____
   _____
   _____

Solution

1. _____
   _____
   _____
   _____
   _____

2. _____
   _____
   _____
   _____
   _____

Reality

_____
_____
_____
_____
_____
_____

Your Declaration

Today, I declare that
I will lead by example in all that I do.
As a parent,
I will commit to modeling the behaviors
I expect to see in my child(ren) through their
conversations, actions, responses,
and behaviors.
As a result,
I my home will promote
a healthy living that is
in alignment with our family values.

James 1:22 ~ But be doers of the word, and not hearers only, deceiving yourselves. **(KJV)**

Tonight as I sit down and reflect on the behaviors I modeled today for my child(ren), I can honestly say

> "Children are our future we must take care of them with maximum effort"
> ~ **Naomi Campbell**

Tonight as I sit down and reflect on the behaviors I modeled today for my child(ren), I can honestly say

Proverbs 14:14 ~ A mean person gets paid back in meanness, a gracious person in grace. **(MSG)**

Tonight as I sit down and reflect on the behaviors I modeled today for my child(ren), I can honestly say

> "I don't want to be a supermodel; I want to be a role model."
> ~ **Queen Latifah**

Tonight as I sit down and reflect on the behaviors I modeled today for my child(ren), I can honestly say

___

Psalm 103:13 ~ As a father shows compassion to his children, so the Lord shows compassion to those who fear him. **(NIV)**

Tonight as I sit down and reflect on my responses or reactions to my child(ren)s' behavior, I can honestly say

_____
_____
_____
_____
_____
_____
_____
_____
_____
_____
_____
_____
_____
_____
_____
_____
_____

> "Children are our future we must take care of them with maximum effort."
> ~ **Naomi Campbell**

Tonight as I sit down and reflect on my responses or reactions to my child(ren)s' behavior, I can honestly say

___

Ephesians 6:4~ And, ye fathers provoke not your children to wrath: but bring them up in the nurture and admonition of the Lord. **(KJV)**

Tonight as I sit down and reflect on the behaviors I modeled today for my child(ren), I can honestly say

_____
_____
_____
_____
_____
_____
_____
_____
_____
_____
_____
_____
_____
_____
_____
_____

Step 6

Take the Time to Teach

"KNOWLEDGE IS POWER."

My Story: Recently, on the way home from school, I started a discussion on faith. My oldest son explained a conversation he was having with a classmate who I sometimes drop off home. The young lady was telling him about how her parents were now separated. Daron then asked the young lady how she felt about the situation and wanted her parents to get back together. The girl replied, "yes," confirming that she did enjoy her parents back together. He responded by recommending that she should pray about it. The young lady replied that prayer does notwork.

He ended the conversation by saying that it does and gave her a supporting example of how prayer can change things. I then realized that he learned what was taught to him to the point that he could apply it and testify to its results. With continuous positive results, my children are now sharing this process with their friends,and that, my friend, is teaching at its best!

Problem: No matter what era we're in, it is still up to the parents to teach their children. I am not sure when it became customary for the world to train up our children in the right path because it is not their job: it is ours. Leaving such a great responsibility to the world at large has been and will continue to be the biggest mistake we have made in history and in time. We are now in an era where all sorts of social media platforms become the teachers for our children and our homes.

Why do I say this? Have you seen the recent changes in education, the churches' issues, and the increased access to several inappropriate social media platforms? If not, tune into your local news station or check out what is feeding your child day in and day out. Check out what type of video games your child is playing. Ask them for their preferred radio station and listen with them. You will be amazed at how quickly they may turn the station because they do not want you to hear certain parts or a specific song in its entirety.

Solution: Teaching a child is a process that requires much patience, consistency, observation, and modeling. It is not something that is achieved overnight! Too often, we focus on when and where our children pick up a lot of the bad habits they have when instead, the focus should also be on what we are teaching or not teaching them. Suppose our children display behaviors or mannerisms that are unacceptable, yet we do not consistently correct them. In that case, we are setting them up for living a chaotic life.

Spend a week just observing what you find inappropriate at the dinner table, during the drive to school, at a family outing, or church. Observe and make the strategic and consistent changes that are necessary. When you notice the behavior or conversation that does not align with your parental values, turn it into a teachable moment for them instead of chastising them. Take that opportunity to reintroduce them to your family values and beliefs as it relates to their behavior. Be willing to answer the "why" questions as well.

Reality: Leaving the parenting to the teachers, the church, and the streets in many cases are not one of the best options to choose. As parents, regardless of age, we are obligated to fulfill our roles in our children's lives. We are our children's first teachers, ministers, leaders, coaches, mentors, and friends. Therefore, we must do our part in teaching our children at home first. This is a special responsibility that we cannot leave for society when setting our children up for success.

As parents, we need to put our children in environments at home that is conducive to positioning them on a successful path. The Bible says to "point your kids in the right direction-when they're old, they won't be lost" Proverbs 22:6 (MSG). In which direction are you pointing your child based on your parenting (teaching) approach? If you aren't happy with your answer, what are you going to do about it? How are you going to get it done? This path will lead them to become healthy, independent, successful, and mature individuals in life.

What's Your Story?

Journal
from the heart

"Teaching a child is a process which takes a lot of patience, consistency, observing and modeling."

~ **Dr. Sindy**

Step 6

Take Time to Teach

"Knowledge is power."

Week 6

Think About This

In which direction are you pointing your child based on your parenting (teaching) approach? Are you happy with the direction your child(ren) is heading? If you aren't happy with your answer, what are you going to do about it? How are you going to get it done? After reflecting on the questions above which deals with taking time to teach, today, sit down in a quiet place and write the top two problems you are facing as it relates to you in this area. Jot down two solutions you are willing to apply immediately to get the results you desire. Then write down what might get in your way from realistically applying the standards you already set in place.

Problem

1. _____
_____
_____
_____

2. _____
_____
_____
_____

Solution

1. _____
_____
_____
_____

2. _____
_____
_____
_____

Reality

_____
_____
_____
_____
_____
_____

Your Declaration

Today, I declare
that being my child(ren)
first teacher, mentor and coach
is not a challenge for me.
As a parent,
I commit to educating
my child(ren) in a manner
that promotes,
love, understanding and respect.
As a result,
our family unit will be built in
alignment with our family values.

 **Day 1**

> **Proverbs 22:6** ~ Train up a child in the way he should go; even when he is old he will not depart from it.
> **(KJV)**

Tonight as I sit down and reflect on how I taught my child(ren), I can honestly say that my actions

_____
_____
_____
_____
_____
_____
_____
_____
_____
_____
_____
_____
_____
_____
_____
_____
_____
_____

"At torn jacket is soon mended, but hard words bruise the heart of a child."
~ **Henry Wadsworth Longfellow**

"Tonight as I sit down and reflect on how I taught my child(ren), I can honestly say that my actions

___
___
___
___
___
___
___
___
___
___
___
___
___
___
___
___

> **Proverbs 10:11** ~ The mouth of a good person is a deep, life-giving well, but the mouth of the wicked is a dark cave of abuse. **(MSG)**

Tonight as I sit down and reflect on how I taught my child(ren), I can honestly say that my actions

> "[Kids] don't remember what you try to teach them. They remember what you are."
> ~ **Jim Henson**

Tonight as I sit down and reflect on how I taught my child(ren), I can honestly say that my actions

Day 5

Proverbs 10:32 ~ The speech of a good person clears the air; the words of the wicked pollute it. **(MSG)**

Tonight as I sit down and reflect on how I taught my child(ren), I can honestly say that my actions

"Those who know, do. Those that understand, teach."
~ **Aristotle**

Tonight as I sit down and reflect on how I taught my child(ren), I can honestly say that my actions

> **Proverbs 15:7** ~ The lips of the wise disperse knowledge, but the heart of the fool does not do so. **(NKJV)**

Tonight as I sit down and reflect on how I taught my child(ren), I can honestly say that my actions

___

Step 7

Take the Time to Support

"Lean on me."

My Story: During the elementary school performance at my son's school, I was surprised to see one of them upfront and singing. To be honest, I never knew that sound existed in my son. In my eyes, he was a shy young man who was afraid of engaging with other students. However, that was not the case. Not only does he have an incredible voice, but he also has many other talents. I was pleasantly surprised at the level of confidence my son displayed during the performance.

For a long time, I focused solely on ensuring my sons' basic needs were always made available as a parent. Although family time and family outings took place, I still missed discovering his hidden talents. I assumed that what I saw on a day-to-day basis was it. Boy, was I wrong. Although I would talk to him and have great discussions, I honestly never thought about discussing talents. As a result, he may have thought I'd never support his musical talents and kept it hidden from me. Whatever the reason for my son not sharing, it was a part of him I had to learn about through his school instead of directly.

Problem: Life demands can rob us (parents) of the opportunity to really engage with or even support our children's goals, dreams, or aspirations. This limits us only with the opportunity to focus solely on the basic needs of our children, subsequently forcing us to neglect the other activities that would require more from us. Believe me; I get it. The expectation for us to operate on autopilot as though we are robots is real. However, that is not how we are wired. We are created to feel every single emotion, whether good or bad.

If this true for us, then so it is for our children. They desire to be heard, supported, and engage in activities or discussions that they like or believe are important to them. Not being supported at home leaves them searching for support elsewhere, regardless if the support is negative or positive. This, in return, can lead to conflicts in th house that could have been avoided.

Solution: Find out what are their challenges, likes, or interests are and support them. During this discussion, take a mental note of your findings. Once you gather your information, carefully process what you have learned to further engage in future discussions with them. This will serve as a tool that you can use to resolve any present or past issues. If there is a sport or a talent they want to develop, support them the best way you know-how. If you or trustworthy family members cannot support them, look within your community to see if mentorship programs will meet those needs. Make an effort to discover free resources that will help you become more supportive without exhausting your finances. There are free magazines such as Parent Magazine, online communities filled with information on discovering ways to support your child effectively. Regardless of whether the sites are in your local city or state, the information and resources are universal.

Reality: If we do not take the time to engage with and support our children, there will be an inevitable disconnect in the family unit. Children have a way of showing their talents through their behaviors early in life. But if they are ignored, not supported, and not appropriately nurtured, those talents can become underdeveloped. You could potentially miss out on an essential piece of your child's life simultaneously, missing the opportunity to support or even discover your child's hidden talents. Are there hidden talents your child has that you have not supported? Are there activities that your child has interests in that you have not noticed? What are you going to do to support your child? It is equally vital for us as parents to support our child's skills, even those outside of the realms of academics and or athletics.

What's Your Story?

Journal

from your heart

"If we do not take the time to engage with and support our children, there will be an inevitable disconnect in the family unit."

~ Dr. Sindy

Step 7

Take Time to Support

"LEAN ON ME"

Week 7

Think About This

Are there hidden talents your child has that you have not supported? Are there activities that your child has interests in that you have not noticed? What are you going to do to support your child? It is equally important for you (the parent) to support all of your child's talents even those outside of the realms of academics and or athletics. After reflecting on the questions above which deals with taking time to support, today, sit down in a quiet place and write the top two problems you are facing as it relates to you in this area. Jot down two solutions you are willing to apply immediately to get the results you desire. Then write down what might get in your way from realistically applying the standards you already set in place.

Problem

1. _____
   _____
   _____
   _____

2. _____
   _____
   _____
   _____

Solution

1. _____
   _____
   _____
   _____

2. _____
   _____
   _____
   _____

Reality

_____
_____
_____
_____
_____
_____
_____

Your Declaration

Today, I declare that
I take pleasure
in supporting my child(ren).
As a parent,
I commit to taking advantage of all
opportunities available to support them
academically, socially, financially or spiritually.
As a result,
our focus is on creating lasting memories
today and for years to come.

Psalm 20:2 ~ May he send you help from the sanctuary and grant you support from Zion. **(NIV)**

Tonight as I sit down and reflect on how I supported my child(ren), I can honestly say that I

___
___
___
___
___
___
___
___
___
___
___
___
___
___
___
___

Day 2

> "If you want to support others you have to stay upright yourself."
> ~ **Peter Høeg**

Tonight as I sit down and reflect on how I supported my child(ren), I can honestly say that I

Day 3

> **Ezra 10:4** ~ Rise up; this matter is in your hands. We will support you, so take courage and do it. **(NIV)**

Tonight as I sit down and reflect on how I supported my child(ren), I can honestly say that I

Day 4

> "Support and encouragement are found in the most unlikely places."
> ~ **Raquel Cepeda**

Tonight as I sit down and reflect on how I supported my child(ren), I can honestly say that I

Psalm 54:4 ~ Surely God is my help; the Lord is the one who sustains me. **(NIV)**

Tonight as I sit down and reflect on how I supported my child(ren), I can honestly say that I

> "Every person needs support from others to be able to reach his/her dreamland."
> ~ **Euginia Herlihy**

Tonight as I sit down and reflect on how I supported my child(ren), I can honestly say that I

Psalms 121:2 ~ My help comes from the Lord, the Maker of heaven and earth. **(NIV)**

Tonight as I sit down and reflect on how I supported my child(ren), I can honestly say that I

Step 8

Take the Time to Validate

"I APPROVE THIS MESSAGE."

My Story: My younger son never liked or had a desire to eat vegetables. My God, it was even a mission to get him to eat any sort of vegetables, even on his burgers. Regardless of how I tried to convince him that eating vegetables was good for him, it ended with me feeling frustrated, defeated, and annoyed. No matter how much I yelled, shouted, and even threaten to take his dessert away, this was simply a temporary relief to the dilemma. Eventually, I realized that this was not working, and I needed to develop another game plan. I then decided that I would reward him and share how proud I was of him eating a few vegetables. I did this consistently for a while until he eventually began to eat more vegetables on his own.

You see, he realized that I was now focused on him making an effort compared to not making an effort. Suddenly, he realized that I acknowledged that he did not like vegetables but was proud that he was making an effort to eat them. He saw that I celebrated the little he did, which made him want to do it again. One day, his older brother shared with us that his younger brother began choosing to eat salad on his own at school. When I found out, I celebrated his decision even more.

Problem: First, let us understand that there are two types of validation. One is positive, while the other is negative. Regretfully, some parents believe that the best kind of validation is the harmful kind as a form of reverse psychology. I have witnessed parents responding or validating behaviors they dislike without even realizing it. You've seen it at times when the trash has not been taking outside. The dishes are still dirty or when they are playing video games instead of doing homework. How is this validation, you might ask? Whatever actions we react to instead of responding to the most are what we are validating. If the only response he/she receives comes from negative behaviors present, that is, the action will ultimately be repeated.

Solution: Start replacing the negative validations with positive ones. Focus on those behaviors aligned with what you hold to be true at home, given they would yield positive results. What does that mean? Find those positive actions or behaviors within your child and continue to validate them consistently. How? Express to them how you appreciate, love, or notice their efforts immediately upon seeing it. Reward them with high-fives, hugs, kisses, or even their favorite ice cream. Do something that will allow them to experience the joy of being noticed and rewarded for deciding to do the right thing. You will be surprised at the instant results.

Reality: The reality of it all is this: if we continue to validate the behaviors we disapprove of in the home, we will unintentionally cause them to repeat such actions. Society does a great job validating all those negative behaviors consistently. This is why juvenile detention centers are never empty. The cop cars are always filled with our children, and sadly, the graveyards are filling up quickly. After reading this, which form of validation, can you identify that is most consistent in your home? Is it positive or negative? If it is negative, how are you going to change it?

What's Your Story?

Journal
from the heart

"Find those positive actions or behaviors your child is displaying and consistently validate them."

~ **Dr. Sindy**

Step 8

Take Time to Validate

"I APPROVE THIS MESSAGE"

Week 8

Think About This

There are two forms of validation. One is positive while the other is negative. Which form of validation can you identify that is most consistent in your home? Why do you believe this form of validation is more consistent in your home? If it is negative, how are you going to change it? After reflecting on the questions above which deals with taking time to validate, today, sit down in a quiet place and write the top two problems you are facing as it relates to you in this area. Jot down two solutions you are willing to apply immediately to get the results you desire. Then write down what might get in your way from realistically applying the standards you already set in place.

Problem

1. _____
   _____
   _____
   _____

2. _____
   _____
   _____
   _____

Solution

1. _____
   _____
   _____
   _____

2. _____
   _____
   _____
   _____

Reality

_____
_____
_____
_____
_____
_____

Your Declaration

Today, I declare
that I will no longer validate the negative
behaviors displayed by my child(ren).
As a parent,
I commit to responding more to
them in a manner
that promotes,
love, understanding and respect.
As a result,
I will express my appreciation immediately
to those behaviors that
are in alignment with our family values.

Matthew 11:28 ~ Come unto me, all ye that labor and are heavy laden, and I will give you rest. **(KJV)**

Tonight as I sit down and reflect on my child(ren)s' behaviors, I can honestly say that validated or responded

> "To encourage me is to believe in me, which gives me the power to defeat dragons."
> ~ **Richelle E. Goodrich**

Tonight as I sit down and reflect on my child(ren)s' behaviors, I can honestly say that validated or responded

_____
_____
_____
_____
_____
_____
_____
_____
_____
_____
_____
_____
_____
_____
_____
_____
_____
_____
_____
_____
_____

Psalm 139:14 ~ "I will praise thee; for I am fearfully and wonderfully made: marvelous are thy works; and that my soul knoweth right well." **(KJV)**

Tonight as I sit down and reflect on my child(ren)s' behaviors, I can honestly say that validated or responded

___
___
___
___
___
___
___
___
___
___
___
___
___
___
___
___
___

> "Fly to where your heart takes you. He who waits for the approval of others has clipped his own wings."
> ~ **Almine**

Tonight as I sit down and reflect on my child(ren)s' behaviors, I can honestly say that validated or responded

___
___
___
___
___
___
___
___
___
___
___
___
___
___
___
___
___
___
___

> **Proverbs 14:26** ~ In the fear of the LORD is strong confidence: and his children shall have a place of refuge." **(KJV)**

Tonight as I sit down and reflect on my child(ren)s' behaviors, I can honestly say that validated or responded

_____
_____
_____
_____
_____
_____
_____
_____
_____
_____
_____
_____
_____
_____
_____
_____
_____
_____
_____
_____

# Day 6

> "When you learn to talk people up, you will never talk yourself down."
> ~ **Richmond Akhigbe**

Tonight as I sit down and reflect on my child(ren)s' behaviors, I can honestly say that validated or responded

Colossians 3:21 ~ Fathers, do not embitter your children, or they will become discouraged. **(NIV)**

Tonight as I sit down and reflect on my child(ren)s' behaviors, I can honestly say that validated or responded

Step 9

Take the Time to Invest

"I AM WORTH IT."

My Story: I am fortunate to have children that are both musically and athletically talented. Like most typical youth, they also love all sorts of electronics, especially gaming systems. When they were younger, I invested in games and toys that incorporated some educational component. As they got older in age, IRONICALLY, they were no longer interested in educational toys or games solely.

They were now fascinated with the race cars and athletic types of games. Grant it, they had none of these games at home, but their friends at school, in church, or their cousins had a plethora of games. I did not approve of some of the ones like the killing, shooting, fighting, or pornographic themed cartoon games. Because of this realization and because they begged me repeatedly, I decided to invest in some games for them. However, they had to earn it by working hard to maintain good grades in school each quarter.

I made sure my sons understood the game they were going to receive was a direct result of their hard work. I made sure they understood for them to continue having the privilege to use it based on their continued academic performance. You see, I invest a lot in ensuring they have quality education and their athletic and musical talents. But because they are maturing and deserve it as they met my standards, I invested in fulfilling their want of a gaming system.

Problem: In this day and age, it is customary to see parents investing in all sorts of electronics, apparel, footwear, hairstyles, and more for their children. Every year during this popular holiday called Black Friday, all social media platforms are filled with stories. People expressed how long they had to wait for the new electronic device, game, apparel, or sneakers because of the great discounts or deals they are guaranteed to receive. Regretfully, this same media coverage trend of parents camping out or waiting in long lines to get their child enrolled at the best elementary school is unheard of. Neither have I ever heard of parents waiting overnight at the school to pick up their child's latest report card.

What do I mean? Through my nineteen years of working with students, regardless of if it was in a secondary, post-secondary, or ministry level, I have witnessed many things. I saw children rocking the newest clothes, shoes, everything. Yet, they could not read, write cursive, complete a simple form correctly, pray, and more. When the time came for parent conferences or to get much-needed information from them to complete or update their child's file at the school, the responses were low, regretfully.

Now, I am not saying that investing in the latest gaming system, shoes, apparel, are wrong. On the contrary, it is a good reward as long as it is connected to behaviors that align with your home's values. This will translate to them that they must invest their own time and effort to earn those things they want, outside of what they need.

Solution: There are so many ways you can invest in your child. Spending time with your children can be a rewarding and fulfilling experience as it once was before. Do you remember when your child was a toddler around the age of two or three years old? Can you hear their laughter and excitement when they played in the park or outside as you watched them? What about when you took them to their first theme park with rides? Just as they were excited back then hanging out with you, that feeling of excitement can be experienced now regardless of how old they are. Get back to investing more of you in hopes of seeing your child smile, sing, dance, or express those emotions of joy as they did before.

Reality: Although we invest in specific technologies such as iPads, iPods, laptops, smartphones, Xbox, Wii, Play Stations, PSPs, or tablets, there are practical ways to investing your time to bonding with your child. I understand that with the high malicious crimes involving children, we as parents feel a need to empower them with some electronic device in case of an emergency. However, more crimes are starting from these same electronic devices we intended our children to use as a safety measure in this day and age.

What used to be the norm for doctors, lawyers, and other individuals in highly demanding careers have now been made available to our children. From infants to adults, I see a trend related to different forms of electronic devices that are available. Suppose we do not find a balance for it all. In that case, our children's capacity to gracefully transition through each developmental stage will become obsolete. Additionally, common social skills will decline as they are now glued to electronics instead of engaging with one another. In what ways have you been investing in your child(ren)? Are you satisfied with the results you are experiencing in this area? If the results are not what you desire, how do you plan to fix it immediately?

What's Your Story?

Journal
from the heart

"Spending quality time with your children can be are warding and fulfilling experience"

~Dr. Sindy

Step 9

Take Time to Invest

"I AM WORTH IT"

Week 9

Think About This

In what ways have you been investing your time in your child(ren) without distractions? Are you satisfied with the results you are experiencing in this area? If the results are not what you desire, how do you plan of fixing it immediately? After reflecting on the questions above which deals with taking time to invest, today, sit down in a quiet place and write the top two problems you are facing as it relates to you in this area. Jot down two solutions you are willing to apply immediately to get the results you desire. Then write down what might get in your way from realistically applying the standards you already set in place.

Problem

1. _____
   _____
   _____
   _____

2. _____
   _____
   _____
   _____

Solution

1. _____
   _____
   _____
   _____

2. _____
   _____
   _____
   _____

Reality

_____
_____
_____
_____
_____
_____
_____

Your Declaration

Today, I declare
that I will find creative ways to
spend time with my child(ren).
As a parent,
I commit to creating family time regularly to promote
love, understanding and respect.
As a result,
the memories we create
will support our family values.

Job 10:12 ~ You gave me life and showed me kindness, and in your providence watched over my spirit. **(NIV)**

Tonight as I sit down and reflect on how I invested time for my child(ren), I can honestly say that today was a

_____
_____
_____
_____
_____
_____
_____
_____
_____
_____
_____
_____
_____
_____
_____
_____
_____

Day 2

> "An investment in knowledge pays the best interest."
> ~ **Benjamin Franklin**

Tonight as I sit down and reflect on how I invested time for my child(ren), I can honestly say that today was a

Day 3

> **Psalm 107:37** ~ They sowed fields and planted vineyards that yielded a fruitful harvest. **(KJV)**

Tonight as I sit down and reflect on how I invested time for my child(ren), I can honestly say that today was a

_____

_____

_____

_____

_____

_____

_____

_____

_____

_____

_____

_____

_____

_____

_____

_____

_____

_____

_____

Day 4

> "Children are our most valuable resource."
> ~ **Herbert Hoover**

Tonight as I sit down and reflect on how I invested time for my child(ren), I can honestly say that today was a

_____
_____
_____
_____
_____
_____
_____
_____
_____
_____
_____
_____
_____
_____
_____
_____
_____
_____
_____

Day 5

Proverbs 20:11 ~ Even a child is known by his deeds, whether what he does is pure and right. **(NKJV)**

Tonight as I sit down and reflect on how I invested time for my child(ren), I can honestly say that today was a

_____

> "There can be no keener revelation of a society's soul than the way in which it treats its children."
> ~ **Nelson Mandela**

Tonight as I sit down and reflect on how I invested time for my child(ren), I can honestly say that today was a

Philippians 4:19 ~ And my God shall supply all your need according to His riches in glory by Christ Jesus. **(NKJV)**

Tonight as I sit down and reflect on how I invested time for my child(ren), I can honestly say that today was a

_____
_____
_____
_____
_____
_____
_____
_____
_____
_____
_____
_____
_____
_____
_____
_____
_____

Step 10

Take the Time to Inspire

"Who do I turn to."

My Story: As a parent with many roles, being an inspiration to my children can become a challenge considering all that I do. However, within every position, I find creative ways to include my children through the process. Whether it is when I am attending conferences, teaching, and even writing this book, they are a part of the process. How do I achieve this? By reading the "steps" of this book to them, including them in the photoshoot, or simply asking for their opinion on designs, logos, or even event ideas or concepts, they are included.

You may be wondering how this is inspiring them. By including my sons in the process, I am letting them know that their opinions are worth listening to and are essential to me. Additionally, it allows them to have an active role in my processes. Because of this, they freely promote me everywhere and believe in the My VOICE Matters movement. I inspire them so much that they eagerly share my organization's mission to the neighborhood students to help students with academic, social, and career challenges. They believe in my passion, trust my expertise, and have witnessed the results consistently.

This then moved them from inspiration to investing their allowance to support the movement by purchasing their t-shirts, trinkets, and other promotional materials. They are inspired by my workshops, presentations, seminars, and speaking engagements so much that they pass out my cards to teachers, students, and all those who will listen. All this happened because I decided to include them through the process. Today, they always remind me how I inspire them to do great things when they get older.

Problem: We must realize that inspiration is gained from both inside the home and outside the home. There are commercials, songs, shows, movies, and even behaviors of people that will continuously advertise what they feel are right. Why? Because the goal is to make money irrespective of how damaging it may be to this young generation at large! As a parent, we cannot allow the value of the world to override our own. Your child will look to friends, drugs, social media, or other mediums to inspire them if you do.

Now, some children do not have a home where they are inspired to do the right things. However, I believe there is still hope for them. Undealt or unprocessed pain in children can lead to adverse behaviors later on in life. An article titled Early Drug Abuse Weighs Heavy on Development by Marc D. Gellman, Ph.D., discusses the reasoning behind the use of drugs. It states,"the reason people, ... choose drugs to alter their reality is simply because drugs are '... easily accessible, easy to use, and they are a much easier outlet ...to change the state of feeling."

Solution: Create an environment inside the home that inspires your children. Expose them to people, settings, or experiences you believe will inspire them to become great young adults in the future. Inspire them through encouraging words or by sharing the dreams you once had and were able to attain. Teach them about their family history. And how the opportunities they have can and will open doors that you may not have had opened for you due to the resources made available to them today. Share with them real-life stories of family members who had to deal with the consequences of making the wrong decisions and how that altered their hopes and dreams. Be very honest and open with them.

Reality: We can choose to inspire our children positively or negatively. Again, people, places, and things will fight to encourage your child regardless of how we feel. No one gives birth to a child to train them to become a failure. No parent aspires for their child to be locked up in jail or killed. However, if our children come home and see the same things they see out in the world, then that is what they will use as inspiration. Again, take the time to inspire your child for greatness because the world's agenda is NEVER going to change their values for you. How we teach or encourage our child(ren) today will positively or negatively impact their adult life. Are you inspiring your child? Can you share an experience when your child expressed this to you? If you cannot answer truthfully, what steps are you going to take to change that? Remember: "train up a child in the way he should go: and when he is old, he will not depart from it" (Proverbs22:6).

What's Your Story?

Journal

from the heart

"We must realize that inspiration can be gained from both inside the home as well as outside the home."

~ **Dr. Sindy**

Step 10

Take Time to Inspire

"WHO DO I TURN TO?"

Week 10

Think About This

How you teach or inspire your child(ren) today will impact their adult life either positively or negatively tomorrow. Are you an inspiration to your child? Can you share an experience when your child expressed this to you? If you cannot answer truthfully, what steps are you going to take to change that? After reflecting on the questions above which deals with taking time to inspire, today, sit down in a quiet place and write the top two problems you are facing as it relates to you in this area. Jot down two solutions you are willing to apply immediately to get the results you desire. Then write down what might get in your way from realistically applying the standards you already set in place.

Problem

1. _____
   _____
   _____
   _____
   _____

2. _____
   _____
   _____
   _____
   _____

Solution

1. _____
   _____
   _____
   _____
   _____

2. _____
   _____
   _____
   _____
   _____

Reality

_____
_____
_____
_____
_____
_____
_____
_____

Your Declaration

Today, I declare that no longer will
the world inspire my child(ren) more than me.
As a parent,
I commit to creating experiences for
my child(ren) that promotes,
love, understanding and respect.
As a result,
my child(ren) will see me as their hero,
biggest motivator and supporter.

 **Galatians 6:9** ~ And let us not lose heart in doing good, for in due time we shall reap if we do not grow weary. **(ESV)**

Tonight as I sit down and reflect on how I inspired my child(ren), I can honestly say that today was a

___
___
___
___
___
___
___
___
___
___
___
___
___
___
___
___
___

> "We inevitably doom our children to failure and frustration when we try to set their goals for them."
> ~ **Dr. Jess Lair**

Tonight as I sit down and reflect on how I inspired my child(ren), I can honestly say that today was a

Philippians 4:13 ~ I can do all things through Christ which strengthens me. **(ESV)**

Tonight as I sit down and reflect on how I inspired my child(ren), I can honestly say that today was a

_____
_____
_____
_____
_____
_____
_____
_____
_____
_____
_____
_____
_____
_____
_____
_____
_____

> "Children are apt to live up to what you believe of them."
> ~ **Lady Bird Johnson**

Tonight as I sit down and reflect on how I inspired my child(ren), I can honestly say that today was a

___

1 Peter 5:7 ~ God cares for you, so turn all your worries over to him. **(ESV)**

Tonight as I sit down and reflect on how I inspired my child(ren), I can honestly say that today was a

> "Children aren't coloring books. You don't get to fill them with your favorite colors."
> ~ **Khaled Hosseini**

Tonight as I sit down and reflect on how I inspired my child(ren), I can honestly say that today was a

___

Joshua 1:9 ~ I've commanded you to be strong and brave. Don't ever be afraid or discouraged. **(ESV)**

Tonight as I sit down and reflect on how I inspired my child(ren), I can honestly say that today was a

Step 11

Take the time to Balance

"Can we meet halfway"?

Sindy Augustin

My Story: There are many ups and downs to parenting. No matter how many times you plan or create a to-do list of some sort, this still does not help you at times. Just thinking of or listing to all that goes on in one single day is exhausting. From helping with homework to preparing dinner to plan family time, attending church during the week, listening to the boys share their days' activities, folding clothes, completing our homework is a lot to keep up with. I even became tired, just saying all of this. But we have to make a decision: to either live or start living.

As I began to add more things to our lives as individuals, we became more disconnected as a family unit. When I realized what had happened, I made drastic changes, including disconnecting the cable service and the landline phone service in our home. As a result of these changes, the relationship between us all has strengthened immensely. The boys were now bonding and laughing more with one another. At the same time, the relationship between our family unit strengthened as well.

We began watching some of the hundred movies I purchased over time that we loved. We created movie time, family night, comedy hour, and more. Why? Because we decided to recalibrate our lifestyle to what was necessary. What could be more important than all the multitasking, excessive electronics, and activities that separated us from being a unit? Love, laughter, and creating more memories of us united than us divided became our priority.

Problem: We live in a microwave society that expects us to complete tasks instantly by multitasking. We have moved from focusing on one thing at a time to doing many things at once. No longer are we concerned with the quality of living. Instead, we are concerned with the quantity of doing. Regretfully, children have adopted this approach and made it a routine. This could mean two or three different sports, jobs, volunteer activities, and so on. Because of the norm of "more," the value of "one" is becoming more and more obsolete. As a result, we see the relationship between parent and child fading away.

Solution: Find the time to reconnect without all the extra stuff. Find the time to create and engage in activities that unite the family instead of separating the family. Consider eating dinner or breakfast together or forming a weekly family night. Read a book together. Play cards or board games with each other. Play outside, build sandcastles, create makeshift tents, play basketball, catch, or other age-appropriate activities.

Doing something that invites your child into your world as they invite you into their own is key to balancing life demands outside of the home.

You can even create a family schedule that includes the electronics for about an hour or so. This way, everyone is doing the same activity together as a unit. For assistance or strategies for accomplishing this, I recommend visiting a parenting website full of resources that you will find useful regardless of how old your child is.

Reality: As parents, we have to create an atmosphere at home that adds value to our children's lives, spiritually, emotionally, physically, financially, nutritiously, academically, mentally, and socially. When we focus on one more than the other, unhealthy behaviors may develop. And that, my friend, is NOT GOOD. Like we need to eat a balanced breakfast or meal, it is with having a balanced home. What can you do TODAY to add structure to your home? What steps are you going to take to ensure your children are active participants in creating and maintaining this structure?

What's Your Story?

Journal
from the heart

"Find the time to reconnect and engage in activities that unite the family instead of separating it."

~ **Dr. Sindy**

Step 11

Take Time to Balance

"CAN WE MEET HALFWAY?"

Week 11

Think About This

As parents, we are obligated to create an atmosphere at home that adds value to our children's lives spiritually, emotionally, physically, financially, nutritiously, academically, mentally, and socially. Just like we need to eat a balanced breakfast or meal, so it is with having a balanced home. What can you do TODAY to add structure to your home? What steps are you going to take to ensure your children are active participants in creating and maintaining this structure? After reflecting on the questions above which deals with taking time to balance, today, sit down in a quiet place and write the top two problems you are facing as it relates to you in this area. Jot down two solutions you are willing to apply immediately to get the results you desire. Then write down what might get in your way from realistically applying the standards you already set in place.

Problem

1. _____
   _____
   _____
   _____

2. _____
   _____
   _____
   _____

Solution

1. _____
   _____
   _____
   _____

2. _____
   _____
   _____
   _____

Reality

_____
_____
_____
_____
_____
_____
_____

Your Declaration

Today, I declare
that my child(ren) and I will
create a new normal for our selves.
As a parent,
I commit to adding structure to our home in a manner
that promotes,
love, hope and unity.

Proverbs 11:1 ~ A false balance is an abomination to the Lord, but a just weight is his delight. **(ESV)**

Tonight as I sit down and reflect on how I engaged in activities with my child(ren), I can honestly say that today was a

___
___
___
___
___
___
___
___
___
___
___
___
___
___
___
___
___

> "Life is like riding a bicycle. To keep your balance you must keep moving."
> ~ **Albert Einstein**

Tonight as I sit down and reflect on how I engaged in activities with my child(ren), I can honestly say that today was a

1 Peter 3:17 ~ take care that you are not carried away with the error of lawless people and lose your own stability. **(ESV)**

Tonight as I sit down and reflect on how I engaged in activities with my child(ren), I can honestly say that today was a

"In all aspects of our lives balance is key. Doing one thing too much can cause upset, like the old saying goes, everything in moderation is the secret!"
~ **Catherine Pulsifer**

Tonight as I sit down and reflect on how I engaged in activities with my child(ren), I can honestly say that today was a

> **Hebrews 11:6** ~ And without faith it is impossible to please him **(ESV)**

Tonight as I sit down and reflect on how I engaged in activities with my child(ren), I can honestly say that today was a

_____
_____
_____
_____
_____
_____
_____
_____
_____
_____
_____
_____
_____
_____
_____
_____

Day 6

> "Work, love and play are the great balance wheels of man's being."
> ~ **Orison Swett Marden**

Tonight as I sit down and reflect on how I engaged in activities with my child(ren), I can honestly say that today was a

Philippians 1:6 ~ that he who has began a good work in you will bring it to completion at the day of Jesus Christ. **(ESV)**

Tonight as I sit down and reflect on how I engaged in activities with my child(ren), I can honestly say that today was a

_____

_____

_____

_____

_____

_____

_____

_____

_____

_____

_____

_____

_____

_____

_____

_____

_____

_____

Step 12

Take the Time to Unite

"UNITED WE STAND, DIVIDED WE FALL."

My Story: My children love sports and enjoy working out. I am a gym or workout fanatic who enjoys working out in a group setting and alone at times. Why? For me, it is my "me time" for escaping the realities of the world while at the same time using the opportunity to stay healthy. I began working out more, and my sons saw me taking my health a lot more seriously than before. Because of this, they requested to join me, and I allowed them to for about a week. Having the children with me was fun in the beginning, but it was not the same. As a result, I no longer allowed them to join me as I worked out.

I could tell that this did not make them happy because they enjoyed our family workouts. I decided to create a family workout time into our schedule, which allowed us to work out together and unite. We were also able to make healthy competition which had its rewards. I did not have to stop what I loved doing. On the contrary, I had to find a way to include them in the picture. We are not only uniting as a family, but we are becoming healthier as a unit,and that is beautiful!

Problem: Living in the same house as your children do not guarantee you are uniting with them. An outpour of cases is frequently displayed on media outlets of families at odds with one another.

Additionally, we see children either physically or verbally fighting with their parents and vice versa. We see both parties working against one another instead of working in partnership with each other.

Yelling is not a useful mode of communication because it can put the child and or the parent in a defense state. It also pushes each party farther apart instead of bringing them close. As a result, the ability to establish trust and respect between parent and child is never actualized. Every household may not be the same, nor share the same experiences. However, you know the challenges you are currently dealing with inside of your home.

Solution: Find ways to connect. Discover what similarities you share and engage in those activities together. Do know that this is not an easy task because it takes time, patience, and determination to unite. Instead of watching what you want to watch as a parent, watch what they are interested in (so long as it is appropriate). The same approach should be applied to music. Listen to what they are listening to and make it a learning experience for both you and your child. Like I said, get into their world.

Suppose you are not willing to see what they are interested in. In that case, you miss out on a great opportunity to bond, educate, inspire, and unite with your child. Here is a great website that can help you find creative and practical ways to collaborate with your child: http://childparenting.about.com/od/lifeathome/a/familyschedule.htm.

Reality: Until we as parents take the path to discover our children without being judgmental, religious, or pessimistic, we will never unite or live in harmony with them. They will continuously see us as the enemy or the person out to make their lives miserable or uninteresting, when, in fact, it is the complete opposite that is true. Unite with them as you both journey into each other's world. The more you take an interest in their world without being judgmental, the more receptive your son or daughter will become as they join your world as their parent. Reflect on how you are currently developing ways to unite with your children. If you cannot, what are you going to do differently? When will you change your current situation? How do you plan on changing it?

What's Your Story?

Journal

from the heart

"Until we as parents take the path to discovering our children without being judgmental, religious, or pessimistic, we will never unite or live in harmony with them."

~ **Dr. Sindy**

Step 12

Take Time to Unite

"UNITED WE STAND, DIVIDED WE FALL"

Week 12

Think About This

The more you take interest in their world without being judgmental, the more receptive your son or daughter will become as they join your world as their parent. Reflect on how you are currently developing ways to unite with your children. If you cannot, what are you going to do differently? When will you change your current situation? How do you plan on changing it? After reflecting on the questions above which deals with taking time to unite, today, sit down in a quiet place and write the top two problems you are facing as it relates to you in this area. Jot down two solutions you are willing to apply immediately to get the results you desire. Then write down what might get in your way from realistically applying the standards you already set in place.

Problem

1. _____
   _____
   _____
   _____

2. _____
   _____
   _____
   _____

Solution

1. _____
   _____
   _____
   _____

2. _____
   _____
   _____
   _____

Reality

_____
_____
_____
_____
_____
_____
_____

Your Declaration

Today, I declare
that no longer will my child(ren)
and I be divided against each other.
As a parent,
I commit to uniting with
my child(ren) in a manner
that promotes,
love, respect and wholeness.
As a result,
the gap between me and my child will
no longer exist.

BRIDGING THE GAP: 12 WAYS TO CONNECT WITH YOUR CHILD

Mark 3:25 ~ If a house is divided against itself, that house cannot stand. **(NIV)**

Tonight as I sit down and reflect on how I united with my child(ren), I can honestly say that today was a

> "All happy families resemble each other, each unhappy family is unhappy in its own way."
> ~ **Leo Tolstoy**

Tonight as I sit down and reflect on how I united with my child(ren), I can honestly say that today was a

> **Ephesians 4:3**~ Endeavoring to keep the unity of the Spirit in the bond of peace. **(KJV)**

Tonight as I sit down and reflect on how I united with my child(ren), I can honestly say that today was a

 **4**

> "The strength of a family, like the strength of an army,
> is in its loyalty to each other."
> ~ **Mario Puzo**

Tonight as I sit down and reflect on how I united with my child(ren), I can honestly say that today was a

_____

_____

_____

_____

_____

_____

_____

_____

_____

_____

_____

_____

_____

_____

_____

_____

 **Amos 3:3**~ Can two walk together, except they be agreed? **(KJV)**

Tonight as I sit down and reflect on how I united with my child(ren), I can honestly say that today was a

> "The Family is the Country of the heart."
> ~ **Giuseppe Mazzini**

Tonight as I sit down and reflect on how I united with my child(ren), I can honestly say that today was a

___
___
___
___
___
___
___
___
___
___
___
___
___
___
___
___
___
___
___
___

> **Romans 14:19**~ Let us therefore follow after the things which make for peace, and things wherewith one may edify another. **(KJV)**

Tonight as I sit down and reflect on how I united with my child(ren), I can honestly say that today was a

___

Conclusion

Being a parent can become challenging when the parent has expectations that may appear unrealistic or unattainable to the child. Unfortunately, this may lead to arguments and disconnection in the family unit. As a result, it can leave the parent asking themselves or saying to their child:

"Is that my child?"

"Where did this one come from?"

"Where did I go wrong?"

"I regret ever giving birth to you."

"I should have waited before having children."

"What was I thinking?"

"I hate you."

"I would have been better off without having you."

These are emotions or feelings usually expressed when challenges arise that leave parents stuck in a place of hopelessness and despair. With every developmental stage children journey into, parents must discover new ways of commending and supporting them. Over time, this will allow parents to master what worked and change what did not. Trust me when I say this process can be the most difficult when the parenting style fluctuates or is not consistent over time. Regardless of how frustrating it may become over time, you (the parent) have to stick with it if you desire your house to become a home.

I am not telling you what I think; I tell you what I've experienced over time. It was a journey I had to take. I had no choice but to apply these same steps in my home. Knowing that I was hopeful of what tomorrow had in store for us all, I had to focus. Seeing my sons grow into responsible young men who could think critically and make the right decisions even when I am not around was necessary. There were times when I was way off, while others I was right on target. Regardless of where I was, I continued to work at it. Why? Because parenting is a journey worth traveling regardless of its detours.

I pray that this book provided you with much-needed steps to resolve the very present challenges you may be facing as a parent. I pray that my Story has provided you with real, thought-provoking applications for solutions to those challenges. I pray this book opens your mind to see more clearly and ignites that desire to take the time needed to connect with your child. Children are not always adequately equipped to make healthy decisions, frequently because they go along with what ever seems right at that particular moment. I pray that you take action just as I did so that you can share what you did to achieve success later in the future despite the challenges of life!

Effective communication, active listening, and taking the time to focus and learn about our child are critical. It is essential to provide a better understanding of the seasons of their life and become that model they need to transition successfully through each developmental stage. As you (the parent) teach them the ways of life and engage in activities that bring them together, doors will open like never before. These doors will help you support your child as the parent to invest your time, love, and life as you watch them grow up is priceless. There is joy in connecting with your child in their elementary stages of life and envisioning them as successful individuals in their community, and the world is gratifying. This can only happen if you take the time to inspire them to be their best. Why? Living a balanced life both inside and outside the home is essential. However, becoming a united family on a mission to conquer every life stage is a journey worth taking. Be intentional and consistent in applying the 12 Ways to Connect With Your Child because it will close any gap that may form in between the family dynamic. Remember, I invite you to partner with you process as you chart a new path of family principles for the generations to come.

About The Author

Dr. Sindy Augustin is the Founder and President of Global Youth Empowerment Movement Inc. and Youth for Prosperity, Inc., a 501c(3) organization. She specializes in educating, inspiring, and elevating participants organically, through resources and tools geared to assist with charting new paths of success, reuniting homes while reshaping the community. Her energetic techniques make learning practical, memorable, fun, and real, catering to all learning styles. Moving client's from confusion to clarity is her desired goal. Sindy's dedication to this message for over 18 years has encouraged students to rewrite the scripts that threaten their intended goals.

Global Youth Empowerment Movement was established in 2009 with the youth in mind. Sindy knew God was getting ready to do great things through her not just locally but globally as well. Her love of philanthropy, compassion for the lost, and vision for a better tomorrow, in addition to GYEM, she established Youth for Prosperity. As an educator of over 19 years, Dr. Sindy established Sindy Speaks Global; an educational and training firm that helps parents and educators uncover roadblocks so that the student can achieve maximum success. Through the many partnerships and initiatives aimed to impact the lives of youth globally, she has a proven track record of having a positive impact on the lives of many.

Since the age of 17, when Dr. Sindy gave her life to Christ, she always devoted her time and talent to help the youth in her community. Though her struggles were many, Sindy never allowed them to dictate her tomorrow. She never gave in to defeat and despair. Because of her resiliency, she accomplished her educational dreams amid adversity. With every challenge along her educational journey, she pushed through it all. She achieved her academic pursuits in earning her Doctors Degree in Educational Leadership K – 12 from Lynn University. Even though her degree took longer than she anticipated, it did not stunt her will, desire, and push to finish strong.

Hope is what drove her to see the possibilities believe the unimaginable and take risks like none other. Her Story catalyzes change for youth. As a result, Dr. Sindy has dedicated over 19 years to motivate and educate youth on creating new paths of success for their educational, career, spiritual, and life goals.

Other Titles By Author

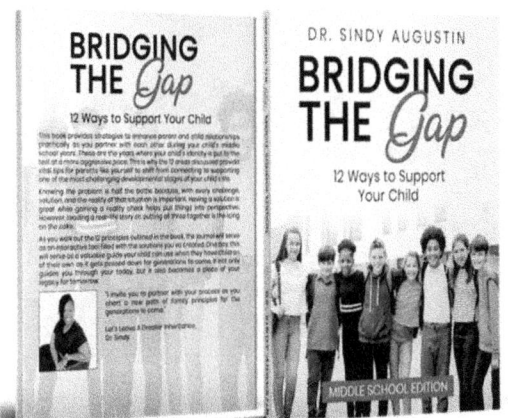

Coming March 2021

Coming June 2021

Coming August 2021

www.ingramcontent.com/pod-product-compliance
Lightning Source LLC
Chambersburg PA
CBHW081408080526
44589CB00016B/2505